THE LITTLE MEDITERRANEAN COOKBOOK

HOW TO COOK SIMPLE MEDITERRANEAN DISHES FROM SPAIN

BY

VANESA MAZA

The Little Mediterranean Cookbook - How to cook simple
Mediterranean dishes from Spain
by Vanesa Maza

First published 2021
© Copyright 2021 by Vanesa Maza – All rights reserved
Photography copyright © Vanesa Maza
Edited by José Tavares

DEDICATION

This cookbook is lovingly dedicated to my papa Julio, who taught me most of the recipes in this book, to my mum Ivonne, my sister Graciela and my cousin José Luis who helped me with the photos and to my boyfriend Matt who helped with the tasting.

TABLE OF CONTENTS

INTRO

Discover Spanish Mediterranean cooking and engage in the culture direct from the comfort of your own kitchen!

In this book I'll share with you some traditional, easy-to-follow recipes that **I've always enjoyed when growing up in between Madrid and Castilla-La Mancha, in Spain**. There's something on the menu for all palettes to enjoy, especially if you want to try something a bit different. If you're stuck wondering what to cook this week, or for a special occasion, you'll find something delicious here.

If you want to surprise someone with authentic Mediterranean cooking in an easy and practical way, then this book is for you! There are some delightfully tasty light options that are perfect for summer, as well as some that are hearty and great for those cold winter evenings.

Basic Essentials The most important way to get maximum flavour is to buy the best ingredients that are as fresh as possible from your local market. The only equipment that I recommend you have is a **blender, a food processor, a pestle and mortar, and some terracotta dishes. A paella pan** is great to have but not entirely necessary as you can use a normal pan.

A bit about me I am from Madrid which is where I grew up and experienced the 'el tapeo' (going out for tapas) lifestyle that is characteristic of Madrilenian culture. In the summer I was lucky enough to spend time at my family's home town in Cuenca, Castilla-La Mancha, a countryside region an hour outside of Madrid. Lots of fond memories were made spending good quality time with friends and family enjoying my papa Julio's cooking.

My papa has always been a man of very few words, however, I have always said that his cooking does the talking for him! That is why I want to bring his recipes to your table so that you and your loved ones can converse through the enjoyment of his recipes from all across the world.

This book is a simple guide to Spanish Mediterranean dishes popular in homes across the whole of Spain. Most of the recipes are from Madrid and Castilla-La Mancha but there are also recipes from other Spanish regions.

Let's Go! Have a go at cooking these simple authentic Mediterranean dishes from the comfort of your home. Invite your friends and enjoy these recipes together! Pick a recipe and start cooking now, everyone's going to absolutely love it. They are *muy buenas! /very good!*

I hope you enjoy the book.

Buen provecho! /Enjoy!

COCINA ESPAÑOLA – SPANISH COOKING

A Background To Spanish Mediterranean Cooking

Many civilizations have conquered or lived in the Spanish peninsula. From the Moors to the Romans, they all contributed to creating what is now the Spanish kitchen, which is also a part of the Mediterranean diet.

The northern regions are colder and more wet than the rest of Spain. They are well known for both fish and seafood from the Atlantic Ocean and Cantabric Sea, as well as good quality cattle, lamb and dairy foods. Their recipes tend to be warming and filling.

The hot regions of the south of Spain, occupied by Moors for 700 years, produce olives and olive oil and they are well known for their fried fish. The east Mediterranean coast of Spain was invaded by the Romans and is the land of herbs, oranges and rice and is renowned for their paellas. Inner Spain is rich and varied and the characteristic dishes are pig roasts, stews and Manchego cheese.

The discovery of the Americas introduced tomatoes, potatoes, chilies and peppers to Spain.

One of the most important ingredients for Spanish cooking is **extra virgin olive oil**. Spain produces about half of the world's olive oil, so I recommend that you use a good quality Spanish olive oil to prepare these recipes. Another important ingredient is garlic, and you'll find this full-flavoured and tasty ingredient in many recipes.

Spanish people also love seafood. When you visit Spain, you'll see a huge **variety of seafood** in the local markets. Let's not forget sausages! The most popular being Chorizo, a pork sausage made with spices such as paprika, and a very popular tapa in the Spanish bars!

Spanish meals are incomplete without **fruit and vegetables**. We always add them to our meals, especially peppers and tomatoes when cooking, or as a salad to accompany the main dish. In Spain it's also very popular to have fruit for dessert. Spanish food is full of flavour which makes fruit a great desert to refresh the palate.

Spain has the third highest life expectancy of any country in the world, which says a lot for our healthy eating habits. We rarely eat fast foods as we generally prefer homemade food much more. Most Spanish families stay away from processed foods and focus more on doing the daily or weekly shopping for fresh ingredients to enjoy the enhanced flavours they bring to their meals.

> *The style of Spanish cooking and its location in the Mediterranean region make it an **integral part of the Mediterranean diet**. Spain shares a similar eating style and good health with other countries in the Mediterranean region, but what probably makes Spain stand out among others is the **"el tapeo"** culture.*

Tapas are the small, tasty dishes that you share with your friends and family. They are so tasty they are sure to create conversations over the flavours amongst friends. Tapas is a social experience more than anything else. This culture extends all over Spain and each region has different varieties.

In some places you get them for free when you order a drink in the bars, especially in central and southern Spain. It's also enjoyed in restaurants and at home. The variety is so extensive that every time you travel to a new place in Spain you can discover a new variety of tapa. The creativity is endless, and the experience is always fun.

Many foodies from around the world travel to Spain, if only to try the wide variety of tapas. A visit to Spain allows you to discover the range of many delicious foods, flavours and wines available that make it the ultimate foodie experience. It keeps them coming back year after year in search of new gastronomic discoveries and to experience first-hand the Spanish way of life.

In my experience Spanish cooking, whether traditional or modern, the dishes are always prepared with love and passion. Spanish cooks not only love feeding people they also want to create a fun and sociable experience with friends and family. **This social connection is known to increase life expectancy, even more so than diet alone.**

TAPAS RECIPES TO AWAKEN YOUR SENSES

I mage you're in Spain on a sunny day having some tapas on the bar's terrace. The weather is lovely and warm, your drink is nicely chilled, and there is a vibrant buzz of atmosphere in the bar and surrounding streets. You are enjoying the delicious tapas that the waiter brings at each drink you order. Each time it's different - *jamón* (cured ham), chorizo or maybe some olives. You feel a gentle breeze and the sun on your face whilst you **enjoy the true flavour of this vibrant centuries-old custom of 'el tapeo'.**

The best part is that this could only be the beginning of the day. These small appetizers are normally eaten before lunch (which in Spain is around 2pm) and you don't need to be in a bar to do so. Us Spaniards also do this whilst preparing our lunch. We get some tapas from the fridge and enjoy these little pleasures with a drink just to get into the happy cooking vibe. We're all in the kitchen, organised to do the different tasks in a friendly and relaxed atmosphere, socialising with our loved ones around the food.

Tapas are meant to be simple appetizers or snacks that take little or no preparation. It's a style of eating and an experience more than anything, which is the essence of Spanish culture. **Wherever you are in the world, when you have tapas - you'll feel that you're in Spain.**

Salud /Cheers!

Sepia al Ajillo - Cuttlefish in Garlic Sauce

Grilled cuttlefish is a simple, rich in flavour tapa that is ideal with parsley and lemon dressing. Healthy and high in protein.

Difficulty: easy
Prep time: 5 min
Cooking time: 10 min
Serves: 4
Special equipment: pestle and mortar

Ingredients

- 4 cuttlefish (fresh or frozen)
- 8 diced cloves of garlic
- 1 teaspoon of coarse salt
- 1 tablespoon of chopped flat leaf parsley
- 3 tablespoons extra virgin olive oil
- juice of 1 lemon
- *alioli* / Garlic Mayonnaise (optional)

For the *alioli*

- 30g mayonnaise
- 1 clove of garlic, crushed

Method

1. Defrost the cuttlefish if you've bought it frozen. Rinse the cuttlefish inside and out well with cold water and remove any outer membrane. Dry with some kitchen paper.
2. Add the garlic, salt, parsley and 2 tablespoons of extra virgin olive oil to the mortar and crush to a paste.

3. Heat a large pan over high heat. Add 1 tablespoon of extra virgin olive oil and when hot add the cuttlefish and cook for 3 minutes on each side.
4. Turn the heat to low and add the garlic mixture from the mortar to the pan and cook the cuttlefish for a further 3 - 4 minutes, turning over halfway through. Be careful not to burn the garlic as it'll go bitter. Remove the pan briefly from the heat if needed.
5. Place the cuttlefish into a serving dish and then drizzle the lemon juice on top.
6. Serve with *alioli* (optional).
7. To make the *alioli* (optional): crush the garlic to a paste in the mortar. Add the crushed garlic to the mayonnaise and stir well. Add to a small bowl and set aside.

Champiñones al Ajillo - Mushrooms in Garlic Sauce

Mushrooms are a great source of antioxidants and fibre. This delicious tapa will add another nice touch to the table.

Difficulty: easy
Prep time: 5 min
Cooking time: 10 min
Serves: 4
Special equipment: pestle and mortar

Ingredients

- 500g chestnut mushrooms
- 8 cloves of garlic, diced
- salt
- pepper
- 1 tablespoon of chopped flat leaf parsley
- 2 tablespoons of extra virgin olive oil
- 3 tablespoons white wine

Method

1. Clean the mushrooms with some kitchen paper.
2. Add the garlic, salt, pepper, parsley and olive oil to the mortar and crush to a paste.
3. Heat a pan over medium heat. When hot add the garlic mixture from the mortar and cook for 2 minutes, being careful not to burn the garlic.
4. Turn the heat to medium/high and add the mushrooms to the pan. Cook for 5 minutes.
5. Add the white wine and continue to cook until the wine is almost completely reduced.
6. Transfer to a serving dish and serve.

Tostadas con Anchoas – Anchovies on Toast

Simple but packed full of flavour! Anchovies on toast are a real treat. They are great to serve at dinner parties, are extremely flavoursome and are high in Omega 3.

Difficulty: easy
Prep time: 10 min
Cooking time:-
Serves: 4

Ingredients

- 1 tin or 100g anchovy fillets
- 4 slices of wholegrain bread (you can also use gluten free)
- 1 teaspoon smoked Spanish paprika (I use La Vera)
- black pepper, to taste

Method

1. Toast the bread.
2. Drizzle the toast with some of the oil from the anchovy tin and sprinkle with smoked paprika.
3. Top the toasted bread slices with the anchovy fillets and gently press them into the toasts.
4. Sprinkle the toast with black pepper.

Boquerones en Vinagre – White Anchovies in Vinegar

Vamonos de tapas – Let's go for tapas! Nothing is more common in Spain, especially in Madrid, than a plate of *Boquerones* marinated in vinegar. They are served in bars as a tapa and seasoned with extra virgin olive oil, garlic and parsley. They are very moreish and are also a great source of Omega-3!

Difficulty: Medium
Prep time: 6 hours
Cooking time:-
Serves: 4
Special equipment: a glass baking dish (don't use metal)

Ingredients

- 450g fresh white anchovy fillets
- white wine vinegar
- coarse salt
- 5 cloves of garlic, finely chopped
- 2 tablespoons of finely chopped parsley
- extra virgin olive oil

Method

1. Wash the white anchovies in water. If they are not already filleted, cut off the heads, cut open the belly and remove innards. Using your thumb remove the spine and then cut the anchovies into fillets. Rise them under cold water. Place them in a tray and cover with cold water for 30 minutes to get rid of the blood.

2. Discard the water. Rinse the anchovies with fresh water and pat dry with kitchen paper. Place a layer of fillets flat on the bottom of the glass baking dish and sprinkle with salt. Place another layer of fillets on top and sprinkle with salt. Continue laying the remaining fillets and salting, finishing with a sprinkling of salt.

3. Make a mixture of ¾ of vinegar and ¼ of water to cover the fillets and pour over the anchovies. Refrigerate for 4 hours.

4. When finished brining the anchovies discard the vinegar and rinse the anchovies well with cold water. Pat dry with kitchen paper roll and lay the anchovies again in the glass dish.

5. Make a marinade by mixing the garlic and parsley with enough olive oil to cover the anchovies.

6. Pour over the marinade, cover tightly with cling film and refrigerate for 2 to 3 hours.

Langostinos a la Plancha - Grilled King Prawns

These grilled prawns are delicious and super easy to make. They are grilled in the shell with coarse salt and a squeeze of lemon. They make a perfect appetizer for a special occasion or dinner party.

Difficulty: easy
Prep time: 5 min
Cooking time: 10 min
Serves: 4

Ingredients

- 20 king prawns
- 1 lemon, sliced
- 2 tablespoons of finely chopped flat leaf parsley
- 2 tablespoons of extra virgin olive oil
- coarse salt

Method

1. Add the extra virgin olive oil to a large pan on high heat. Once hot, add a layer of prawns to the pan and cook.
2. When the bottom of the prawns is golden sprinkle with a pinch of coarse salt and flip them over to cook the other side. Sprinkle again with a pinch of salt.
3. Once done remove and set aside in a warm dish. Continue cooking the remaining prawns, in batches if needed.
4. Serve with a sprinkling of parsley and lemon slices.

Gambas al Ajillo - Prawns in Garlic Sauce

Gambas al ajillo is one of the most popular tapas across the south coast of Spain. This traditional dish is great for a quick tapa full of garlic flavour!

Difficulty: easy
Prep time: 5 min
Cooking time: 10 min
Serves: 4
Special equipment: a terracotta dish

Ingredients

- 250g frozen, peeled prawns
- 5 finely diced cloves of garlic
- 2 chilies
- 5 tablespoons of extra virgin olive oil
- black pepper
- sea salt
- wholegrain or gluten free bread

Method

1. Defrost the prawns by placing them in the fridge the night before.
2. Rise them with cold water and dry them with kitchen paper.
3. Add the extra virgin olive oil and the chilli to a terracotta dish on high heat. When hot add the finely diced sliced garlic cloves and cook until golden.
4. Remove the chili and garlic from the oil to avoid them burning.

5. Season the prawns with sea salt and black pepper and add to the terracotta dish. After a couple of minutes add the garlic and chilli to the prawns and stir to mix the flavours well.
6. Remove from the heat and place the terracotta dish on the table.
7. Serve with bread.

Tip

It is tradition to share the food and to dip the bread into the terracotta dish, but you can serve in individual dishes if you prefer.

Patatas Bravas – Spicy Potatoes

This simple but delicious dish was created in Madrid after potatoes were brought from America and is probably one of the most popular tapas in Spain. I grew up in Madrid and when going out for a drink this is one of the most-served tapas in the bars. The hot and sweet paprika used is what makes this dish so special and it is easy to make.

Difficulty: easy
Prep time: 10 min
Cooking time: 35 min
Serves: 4

Ingredients

For the potatoes:
- 2 large white potatoes
- 180ml extra virgin olive oil
- small handful of flat leaf parsley, chopped

For the Brava sauce
- 60ml extra virgin olive oil
- 1 teaspoon hot smoked Spanish paprika
- 2 teaspoons sweet smoked Spanish paprika
- 1 tablespoon cornflour
- 1 vegetable stock cube dissolved in 60ml of boiling water
- ½ tablespoon of sea salt
- ½ tablespoon of white wine vinegar

Method

1. Peel and wash the potatoes with cold water and dry with kitchen paper. Cut the potato into cubes of about 2 cm.
2. Place the cut potatoes into a bowl and cover with cold water.
3. Heat 60ml of extra virgin olive oil in a small pan. When hot add the olive oil to a bowl. Add the hot paprika, sweet paprika and cornflour to the bowl and mix well to combine.
4. Return the olive oil mixture back to the pan on medium heat. Slowly add the vegetable stock to the oil mixture, constantly stirring with a wooden spoon. Add the sea salt and white wine vinegar and stir until you have a creamy-consistency sauce. Set aside.
5. Drain the potatoes and dry them with a dish cloth or kitchen paper.
6. Add the 180ml of extra virgin olive oil to a large pan on high heat. When the oil is hot, add the potatoes and cook for 20 minutes, or until golden and cooked though.
7. Line a dish or large bowl with a few layers of kitchen paper. Remove the potatoes from the pan using a slotted spoon and place the potatoes into the kitchen paper roll-lined dish to drain the excess oil. Season with sea salt and place the potatoes into a serving dish.
8. Heat the Brava sauce in a pan over low heat stirring constantly for a couple of minutes.
9. Pour the sauce over the potatoes and add a sprinkle of some chopped parsley.
10. Place the dish in the centre of the table so that people can serve themselves.

Lacón a la Gallega - Galician Ham and Potatoes

This Galician style tapa is enjoyed all over Spain. I've always enjoyed the simple but great flavours of cooked ham and boiled potatoes seasoned with coarse salt and Spanish paprika. It is easy to make, and your guests will love the presentation.

Difficulty: easy
Prep time: 10 min
Cooking time: 25 min
Serves: 4

Ingredients

- 200g sliced *lacón* or cooked ham
- 2 large potatoes, peeled and sliced into thick rounds
- 1 tablespoon smoked Spanish paprika
- 4 tablespoons of extra virgin olive oil
- coarse salt

Method

1. Boil the sliced potatoes for 20 minutes, or until done. Drain and arrange them in a layer on a dish.
2. Season with coarse salt and paprika, and drizzle with extra virgin olive oil.
3. Arrange the ham slices on top of the potatoes in a decorated way, drizzle with some more extra virgin olive oil and sprinkle with paprika.

Tip

It is tradition to share the food from a wooden serving dish, but you can use any serving dish if you don't have one.

Chorizos al Vino Blanco - Chorizo with White Wine Sauce

This Spanish tapa is simple and quick to prepare and will add more colour and flavour to your table. Enjoy a little sociable bite before lunch.

Difficulty: easy
Prep time: 5 min
Cooking time: 10
Serves: 4
Special equipment: a terracotta dish

Ingredients

- 200g small smoked chorizos
- 200ml white wine

Method

1. Heat the terracotta dish over high heat. Add the chorizos and cook for a couple of minutes.
2. Reduce the heat to medium and add the white wine. Continue cooking until the wine is well reduced.

SMALL NIBBLES

If you are not in the mood for cooking tapas you can buy these small nibbles ready-made. You only need to find a Spanish shop wherever you live to get the most popular or authentic brands. Alternatively, you can also find them online and get them delivered to you. In Spain we always have the products mentioned in this section in our pantries. They are canned and last a long time so there is no rush to use them. They are great when you have an unexpected visitor or simply when you fancy a healthy snack with little preparation. There is no cooking required, you just add them to a nice serving bowl and enjoy.

Aceitunas Rellenas de Anchoa- Olives Stuffed with Anchovy

Canned anchovy stuffed olives are always in Spanish pantries. It is probably the most common tapa in Spain because it suits all sorts of tastes. If you don't like anchovies, you can always buy the regular olives without anchovy stuffing.

Jamón Iberico- Iberian Ham

Jamón is probably the most globally recognized food of Spanish cuisine. This tasty tapa is the perfect addition to serve at your dinner party and can be prepared in 5 minutes. It is best served at room temperature as it brings out more of the ham flavour!

Almendra Marcona Tostada - Roasted and Salted Marcona Almonds

Marcona almonds are grown and harvested in coastal areas of Spain. They are round and soft and are considered the best almonds in the world. They have great flavour and are high in protein, antioxidant, potassium and magnesium. They are usually roasted with sea salt and you can eat them as a snack or add them to your salads and vegetables.

Mejillones en Escabeche - Pickled Mussels

Escabeche is a traditional method of preserving foods using vinegar. La Mancha is known for its superb, pickled foods and this is a popular way of eating mussels. Mussels are high in beneficial fatty acids and vitamins.

Queso Manchego - Manchego Cheese

Manchego cheese is made in the La Mancha region of Spain from sheep's milk. My favourite is *curado* or cured – normally cured upwards of 4 months. Manchego cheese that has aged for 6 months acquires a unique caramel, nutty flavour.

Berberechos – Cockles

These delicious little cockles are packed in a brine that maintains the true flavour of fresh seafood. Spanish canned seafood really is world-class! All across Spain it is a tradition to offer canned seafood as a delicacy at restaurants and bars. We always have cans at home so that we can enjoy a little tapa before lunch with our family or friends. They are also a great source of Omega 3.

SALADS & SOUP

Having a fresh salad on the table with each meal is a must at meals within Spanish homes. We love the freshness, the aroma and the flavour of the ingredients. Whether you cook meat, fish or a rice main dish, you make a salad and put it on the table for everyone to serve themselves. They are easy to make and provides a bit of extra colour to the table. I particularly like seasoning them with sea salt, black pepper, extra virgin olive oil and lemon juice. You can also swap the lemon juice for any type of vinegar. One of the Spanish favourites is *vinagre de Jerez* (sherry vinegar) and balsamic vinegar.

Ensalada Mediterránea de Atún – Mediterranean Tuna Salad

Tuna salad is the ideal side dish. They are easy to prepare and contain a wide range of fresh crisp vegetables. Serve with a refreshing lemon vinaigrette.

Difficulty: easy
Prep time: 15 min
Cooking time:-
Serves: 4

Ingredients

- ¼ iceberg lettuce, sliced
- 2 tomatoes, diced
- ½ an onion, thinly sliced
- 1 small can (50g) of anchovy stuffed olives
- 1 can of tuna in extra virgin olive oil
- 3 tablespoons of extra virgin olive oil
- juice of 1 lemon
- salt & freshly ground black pepper, to taste

Method

1. Wash the lettuce, dry it with kitchen paper roll and add it to a salad bowl.
2. Add the tomatoes, onion, olives and tuna to the lettuce.
3. Season the salad with salt and pepper and add the extra virgin olive oil and lemon juice.
4. Give it a good mix and serve.

Ensaladilla Rusa - Russian Salad

Ensaladilla rusa is influenced by the popular dish that Belgian chef Lucien Olivier served in his Moscow restaurant around 1860. This dish was so popular that it spread in Europe and all of Spain. You see a simpler and more affordable version of this dish enjoyed as a tapa or side dish in local Spanish bars, at family picnics and at special occasions.

Difficulty: easy
Prep time: 15 min
Cooking time: 20 min
Serves: 4

Ingredients

- 1 red bell pepper, halved, seeded and core removed
- 2 tablespoons of extra virgin olive oil
- 2 large potatoes, peeled and diced
- 2 carrots, peeled and diced
- 2 tablespoons of frozen peas
- 3 eggs
- 2 tablespoons of small capers
- 1 small can or 50g of pitted Manzanilla olives, halved
- 1 can of bonito tuna or white tuna in olive oil, drained
- sea salt to taste
- 1 teaspoon of chopped parsley
- 150g of mayonnaise

Method

1. Preheat the oven to 180° C.

2. Place the red bell pepper halves skin side up on a baking tray. Drizzle with olive oil and season with salt. Bake in the oven for 45 – 60 minutes, or until the skin blackens. Remove from the oven and cover the tray with a kitchen cloth, or cling film, for 10 minutes. Peel the blackened skin from the peppers and cut in strips.

3. Bring some salted water to the boil in a pot. Add the potatoes and carrots and reduce the heat to a simmer. Cook for 15 minutes and then add the peas. Cook for a further 5 minutes. Drain the vegetables into a sieve and cool under running cold water. Set aside.

4. Bring some more water to the boil in the pot and cook the eggs for 5 minutes. Drain and add cold water to the pot to cool the eggs. Peel the eggs and remove the yolks. Set aside the yolks and finely chop the egg whites.

5. Add the potatoes, carrots, peas, chopped egg whites, capers, olives and tuna to a large bowl. Season with sea salt and add the parsley and mayonnaise. Mix all the ingredients together and spoon into a nice serving dish.

6. Slice the egg yolks and scatter over. Artfully garnish with strips of bell pepper and drizzle with extra virgin olive oil.

Ensalada de Bonito con Pimientos de Piquillo - Bonito Tuna with Piquillo Peppers

Bonito del Norte or bonito tuna comes from the northern coast of Spain and its tender texture makes it a delicacy. I love mixing it with piquillo peppers, onion and large good quality tomatoes to create an explosion of refreshing and delicious flavours.

Difficulty: easy
Prep time: 10 min
Cooking time:-
Serves: 4

Ingredients

- 1 can of bonito or white tuna in olive oil
- 2 piquillo peppers, diced
- 4 vine tomatoes, diced
- ½ sweet white onion, diced
- 1 tablespoon of chopped basil
- extra virgin olive oil
- juice of ½ a lemon
- sea salt & freshly ground black pepper to taste

Method

1. Add the tuna, piquillo peppers, tomato, onion and basil to a salad bowl.
2. Season with salt and pepper. Add the lemon juice and drizzle with olive oil.
3. Toss to combine and serve.

Gazpacho – Cold Raw Vegetable Soup

Refreshing, healthy and extremely tasty. This common Andalusian dish is a chilled tomato-based soup with fresh diced peppers, cucumbers and onion on the side to be added. Light starter, full of vitamin C and one of my favourites! Ideal to accompany some of the main dishes in the following chapters.

Difficulty: easy
Prep time: 15 min
Cooking time:- (refrigerate for 1 hour)
Serves: 4
Special equipment: blender or food processor.

Ingredients

- 1kg tomatoes, quartered & core removed
- 1 onion, diced
- 1 green bell pepper, diced
- 1 cucumber, peeled & diced
- 3 tablespoons of extra virgin olive oil
- 3 tablespoons of sherry or red wine vinegar
- 1 teaspoon of salt
- 1 clove of garlic
- 1 teaspoon of cumin

Method

1. To prepare the garnish: add half the onion, half the green bell pepper and half the cucumber to a bowl. Add 1 tablespoon of olive oil, 1 tablespoon of vinegar and salt to taste. Stir together, cover with cling film and refrigerate until needed.

2. Add all of the remaining ingredients to a blender, or food processor, and process until you have a smooth consistency. Strain the gazpacho into a bowl, cover with cling film and refrigerate for 1 hour. The gazpacho may separate in the fridge so give it a stir before serving.
3. Dish the gazpacho into four bowls and top with some garnish. You can also serve the gazpacho in eight small bowls, or glasses, as a tapa.

SIDE DISHES

You can use any of these side dishes with a main dish. Feel free to combine one, two or more of these side dishes with a main course from the fish & seafood or poultry & meat sections. They are mainly vegetable and potato dishes.

Esparragos Trigueros - Grilled Wild Asparagus

Add some green to your main meals with this delicious vegetable. This is a great compliment to main dishes.

Difficulty: easy
Prep time: 5 min
Cooking time: 10 min
Serves: 4
Special equipment: pestle & mortar

Ingredients

- 250g wild asparagus
- 8 cloves of garlic cloves, diced
- 2 tablespoons of extra virgin olive oil
- coarse sea salt & freshly ground black pepper

Method

1. 1. Trim the hard end of the asparagus and clean them with cold water.
2. 2. Add the garlic, olive oil, salt and pepper to the mortar and crush to a paste.
3. 3. Heat a pan over medium heat. Add the paste from the mortar and cook for 2 minutes, being careful not to burn the garlic.
4. 4. Reduce the heat to medium-low heat and add the asparagus to the pan. Cook for a further 5 minutes, or until the asparagus is cooked through.
5. 5. Place into a suitable dish and serve.

Pimientos de Padrón - Padron Peppers

These peppers are the most popular ones in Spain. They come from the Padrón municipality in Galicia, in northwest Spain. They are a special pepper because of their small size and flavour. Occasionally you'll eat one that is very spicy (some say 1 in 30) but it can be very random, you just never know as they all look the same! Padrón peppers are a delicious side dish and perfect with any meat or fish dish as well as with a Spanish omelette. It makes for a very colourful dish and is great as a tapa.

Difficulty: easy
Prep time: 5 min
Cooking time: 5 min
Serves: 4

Ingredients

- 300g padrón peppers
- 50ml of extra virgin olive oil
- flaky sea salt

Method

1. Rinse the peppers with cold water and dry well with a dish cloth.
2. Heat a pan over high heat and add the olive oil. When the oil is hot, add the peppers and sauté until the skin starts to blister and the peppers are soft. Toss or stir occasionally to cook on all sides.
3. Add some kitchen paper to a dish. Remove the peppers and place on the kitchen paper to drain excess oil.
4. Remove the peppers to a serving dish and sprinkle generously with flaky salt.

Pisto Manchego - Sautéed Vegetables

This dish from La Mancha is prepared from vegetables slowly cooked in their own juices. *Pisto* is a great side dish, but you can also have it as a tapa.

Difficulty: easy
Prep time: 10 min
Cooking time: 45 min
Serves: 4

Ingredients

- 4 tablespoons of extra virgin olive oil
- 1 onion, finely diced
- 1 dried chilli
- ½ red bell pepper, finely diced
- ½ green bell pepper, finely diced
- Salt to taste
- 1 aubergine, finely diced
- 1 courgette, finely diced
- 2 cans (400g) chopped tomatoes

Method

1. Heat a pan over medium heat and add the olive oil. Add the onion and cook until softened, stirring occasionally. Add the peppers, a pinch of salt and continue to cook.
2. Crush the chilli using your hands and add to the pan. Continue to cook until the bell peppers are soft.
3. Add the aubergine, courgette and another pinch of salt and continue to cook for a further 10 minutes, or until the aubergines and courgette are soft.

4. Stir in the canned tomatoes and turn the heat down to low. Cool for a further 20 minutes, stirring occasionally.
5. Remove the pan from the heat and spoon the *pisto* into 4 dishes as a side dish. You can also serve it in 8 small dishes as a tapa.

Patatas a la Vinagreta - Potatoes in Vinaigrette

This was my favourite side dish when I was living at home with my parents. My sister and I used to love it when my papa made this for lunch because of its delicious onion and vinaigrette flavours as well as complimenting meat or fish dishes well.

Difficulty: easy
Prep time: 10 min
Cooking time: 45 min
Serves: 4

Ingredients

- 4 potatoes, peeled and diced
- 1 red onion, diced
- Salt to taste
- 120ml of extra virgin olive oil
- 120ml of white wine vinegar

Method

1. Bring some salted water to the boil in a pot. Reduce the heat to medium, add the potatoes and cook for about 20 minutes, or until the potatoes are cooked through.
2. While the potatoes are boiling, dice the onion and add it to a salad bowl.
3. When the potatoes are cooked, drain them and add to the salad bowl with the onion. Add a pinch of salt, the olive oil and vinegar.
4. Mash the potatoes together with the onions and give it a good mix. Taste and add some more salt and vinegar if necessary.

5. Spoon the potatoes into four dishes as a side dish or leave the bowl in the centre of the table so that people can serve themselves.

Patatas a la Cuchifrita - Fried Potatoes with Courgettes & Garlic

This is a filling an and extremely tasty side dish. Easy to make and vegan friendly.

Difficulty: easy
Prep time: 10 min
Cooking time: 45 min
Serves: 4
Special equipment: pestle & mortar

Ingredients

- 4 tablespoons of extra virgin olive oil
- 3 potatoes, peeled & thinly sliced
- sea salt to taste
- 1 courgette, thinly sliced

For the sauce

- 4 cloves of garlic
- 2 dried chilies
- coarse salt, to taste
- freshly ground black pepper, to taste
- 4 tablespoons of extra virgin olive oil
- 4 tablespoons of white wine vinegar

Method

1. Heat a large pan over high heat and add the olive oil. When the oil is hot, add the potatoes and a pinch of salt. Fry the potatoes until golden. Add the courgette and continue cooking. Reduce the heat if necessary.

2. While the potato is cooking prepare the sauce. Add the garlic, chillies, salt and black pepper to the mortar and crush. Add the olive oil and vinegar and mix together to make a sauce.

3. When the potatoes are golden and soft, and the courgettes cooked through, add the sauce from the mortar to the pan. Add a little water to the mortar, stir to collect any residue of sauce remaining and add it into the pan. Continue cooking until the sauce has thickened, gently stirring occasionally.

4. Spoon the potatoes into four dishes as a side dish or place the pan in the centre of the table so that people can serve themselves.

VEGETARIAN DISHES

These are a couple of options for vegetarians or if you need to make something meat free. These dishes can be served as main dishes for either lunch or dinner, as well as served as tapas.

Pisto Manchego con Huevo - Sauteed Vegetables with Egg

Surprise your friends with one of the most popular dishes from La Mancha, in central Spain. A rainbow of colours from different vegetables cooked slowly with fried eggs on top.

Difficulty: easy
Prep time: 10 min
Cooking time: 45 min
Serves: 4

Ingredients

- 6 tablespoons of extra virgin olive oil
- 1 onion, finely diced
- 1 dried chilli
- ½ red bell pepper, finely diced
- ½ green bell pepper, finely diced
- Salt to taste
- 1 aubergine, finely diced
- 1 courgette, finely diced
- 2 cans (400g) chopped tomatoes
- 4 eggs or 8 for tapas

Method

- Heat a pan over medium heat and add 4 tablespoons of olive oil. Add the onion and cook until softened, stirring occasionally. Add the peppers, a pinch of salt and continue to cook.
- Crush the chilli using your hands and add to the pan. Continue to cook until the bell peppers are soft.

- Add the aubergine, courgette and another pinch of salt and continue to cook for a further 10 minutes, or until the aubergines and courgette are soft.
- Stir in the canned tomatoes and turn the heat down to low. Cook for a further 20 minutes, stirring occasionally.
- Add 2 tablespoons of olive oil to a non-stick pan on medium heat and crack the eggs into it. Cook for 3 - 4 minutes, or until the eggs are cooked. Season with salt and pepper.
- Remove the *pisto* from the heat and spoon into 4 dishes as a side dish, each topped with an egg. Try not to break the yolks. You can also serve it in 8 small dishes, each topped with an egg, as a tapa.

Tortilla de Patata - Spanish Potato Omelette

Spanish omelette, or *tortilla* as called in Spain, is usually served in Spanish homes as a main course. I always cook it with onion, but some people prefer it without. This recipe is simple to prepare and everyone loves it! This recipe is great accompanied with *padrón* peppers or a light salad.

Difficulty: easy
Prep time: 10 min
Cooking time: 30 min
Serves: 4

Ingredients

- 120ml extra virgin olive oil
- 4 medium- sized or 3 large potatoes, peeled & thinly sliced
- 1 onion, thinly sliced
- sea salt to taste
- 6 eggs
- 2 tablespoons of extra virgin olive oil
- coarse salt to taste

Method

1. Add 120ml of olive oil to a frying pan on medium heat. When the oil is hot, add the potatoes and onion. Season with sea salt, cover with a lid and leave to cook. Keep an eye on the potatoes to ensure they are not sticking and burning. If necessary, reduce the heat a bit.
2. When the potatoes have softened, lightly crush them with a palette knife. Raise the heat to high to brown the potatoes, being careful not to burn them.

When the potatoes are golden remove the pan from the heat and set aside to cool.

3. Whisk the eggs and a pinch of salt in a bowl.
4. Remove the potatoes from the pan using a slotted spoon so as not to take too much oil with them. Add the potatoes to the bowl with the whisked eggs and mix well.
5. Add 2 tablespoons of olive oil to a clean, smaller frying pan on high heat. When the oil is hot, add the potato and egg mixture to the pan. Immediately lower the heat to medium-low and cook until the mixture has set. Gently shake the pan from time to time to ensure that the omelette does not stick. Use a fork to gently check that the omelette is setting well.
6. After about 3 minutes flip the omelette. Place a plate over the omelette on top of the pan. Hold the plate down firmly, get a tight grip of the handle and in one quick, confident movement, flip the pan upside down so that the omelette ends up on the plate
7. Add a little more olive oil to the now empty pan and when hot slide the omelette back into the pan from the plate. Reduce the heat to medium-low and continue cooking the omelette. You can use the palette knife to maintain the shape. Cook for about 2 minutes, or until the omelette is done.
8. Remove the omelette from the pan and place it on a plate sprinkle with a pinch of coarse salt and enjoy!

Tip

Don't overcook as Spanish omelette is best when the egg is slightly runny in the middle. But if you don't like it that way you can just cook it for a bit longer. You can serve the omelette in quarters to serve 4 people or cut into smaller pieces to serve 8 people as a tapa.

RICES

As you've discovered in the previous sections Spanish cuisine comes in a wide variety of tastes and styles. But, without a doubt, paella is the most popular rice dish for those who want to eat or cook Spanish recipes. It is also many a Spaniards' favourite dish, not only for the great taste, because preparing a rice dish also means it's the weekend and time to get together with friends and family – it's definitely fun time!

There are many varieties and ways of cooking rice in Spain. The recipes change by region as the locals use different ingredients and styles of cooking. It's the little details that make the dishes their own.

Paella Valenciana is the original paella and derives from the East coast of Spain in Valencia. Here they use local ingredients and seasonal vegetables and have a unique style and technique of cooking paella over a fire.

In this section I've included the rice dishes that I like to cook at home. They all use ingredients that are easy to find in local deli's, Spanish shops and also, more than ever, from online shops.

Something that cooks who are not familiar with the cooking of Spanish paellas and rice dishes is the desirability of socarrat. It is a thin, crunchy layer of rice that sticks to the pan and is almost, but not quite, burnt and not at all bitter. This crust is highly valued by paella cooks.

If you don't have a paella pan you can just as easily make rice dishes at home using a large pan, but to make it more authentic you want to get yourself a small paella pan.

These recipes are the way my papa always prepared the rice dishes at home, as do many Spanish households. This is especially true in Madrid, and other big cities and towns, where many people live in flats and don't have an outside space. These recipes are delicious, and their flavours will transport you to the sunny coast of Spain and the memories of sitting on a terrace looking at the beautiful blue sea and smelling delicious seafood and spicy aromas!

Paella de Mariscos - Seafood Paella

This colourful rice dish with mussels, king prawns and squid will make your evening a memorable one. If you don't have a paella pan you can use a large pan instead. If you can, use fresh seafood but frozen will do. If using frozen seafood put it in the fridge to defrost overnight.

Difficulty: easy
Prep time: 15 min
Cooking time: 25 min
Serves: 4
Special equipment: blender

Ingredients

For the seafood stock
- 8 cleaned mussels (we only need 4 but we have more in case they don't open)
- 50ml of white wine
- 4 black peppercorns
- freshly ground black pepper, to taste
- 1 bay leaf
- 2 seafood stock cubes

For the tomato sauce
- 2 garlic cloves
- 1 tomato
- ½ red bell pepper, diced
- pinch of sea salt

For the rice
- 1 dry ñora pepper (optional)
- 3 tablespoons of extra virgin olive oil
- 8 king prawns in the shell, heads removed (keep the heads)
- 200g squid cut into small pieces
- sea salt
- 1 teaspoon *La Vera* smoked paprika powder
- 250g of bomba rice
- ½ g saffron

Method

1. Optional: make some holes in the dry ñora pepper with a sharp knife and soak in warm water.
2. Boil 200ml of water. Add the mussels, white wine, peppercorns, ground pepper and bay leaf to a saucepan and bring to a simmer. Add the boiled water, cover with a lid and simmer for 3 – 5 minutes, or until the mussels open. Don't overcook as the mussels will go rubbery. Remove from the heat and set aside to cool a bit. Lift out the mussels and remove the top half of the shells. Discard any mussels that haven't opened. Set the mussels aside.
3. Strain the mussel cooking liquid into a large jug or saucepan. Crumble in the seafood stock cubes and add enough boiling water to make 600ml of stock. Stir until the stock cubes have dissolved. Set aside.
4. Add all the tomato sauce ingredients to a blender and process until smooth. Set aside.
5. Wash the squid and dry with kitchen paper roll. Cut into small pieces. Set aside.

6. Add 3 tablespoons of extra virgin olive oil to a paella pan, or a large pan, over high heat. Add the prawn heads and sauté for a few minutes, constantly stirring with a wooden spoon to ensure they are nicely browned all over. Squeeze the prawn heads well with the spoon to extract as much flavour as you can from them. Remove the prawn heads from the pan and discard.

7. Add the prawn tails to the pan and cook over high heat for 1 minute on each side. Remove the prawns and set aside.

8. Add the squid to the pan over high heat, season with salt and fry for a minute or two until golden.

9. Reduce the heat to medium. Add the paprika and prepared tomato sauce to the squid and cook for a further 5 minutes.

10. Add the rice and a pinch of salt and stir the rice for a couple of minutes so that the rice absorbs all of the pan flavours.

11. Increase the heat to high and add the prepared seafood stock to the rice. Add the saffron and stir to distribute the rice evenly across the pan.

12. Optional: remove the ñora pepper from the water and place it in the middle of the pan.

13. Once the liquid comes to the boil don't stir the rice again. Cook on medium-high heat for a further 10 minutes.

14. Reduce the heat to medium. Add the mussels and prawns in a decorative way and cook for a further 4 minutes. Reduce the heat to very low and continue to cook for a further 3 minutes. Remember not to stir the rice!

15. Remove the pan from the heat and cover with aluminium foil or a cloth. Set aside for 5 minutes so that the rice continues to be cooked by the steam.

16. Serve the paella in separate dishes or place the pan in the centre of the table so that people can serve themselves.

Tip

Quarter a lemon and place the quarters on the side of the rice dish, or on a small dish, so that people add lemon to their rice if they wish.

Paella Mixta - Mixed Paella

If you can't' make up your mind with whether you want a seafood or a meat paella, you can always have both with this recipe that has chicken, king prawns and mussels. I like to have *Alioli* (garlic mayonnaise) with this paella, as do many Spaniards.

Difficulty: easy

Prep time: 15 min

Cooking time: 25 min

Serves: 4

Special equipment: blender

Ingredients

For the seafood stock
- 8 cleaned mussels (we only need 4 but we have more in case they don't open)
- 50ml of white wine
- 4 black peppercorns
- freshly ground black pepper, to taste
- 1 bay leaf
- 2 seafood stock cubes

For the tomato sauce
- 2 garlic cloves
- 1 tomato
- ½ red bell pepper, diced
- pinch of sea salt

For the rice
- 3 tablespoons of extra virgin olive oil
- 8 king prawns in the shell, heads removed (keep the heads)
- 200g chicken thighs, diced in 2 cm pieces
- sea salt & freshly ground black pepper
- 1 tablespoon of tomato puree
- ½ teaspoon *La Vera* smoked paprika powder
- 200ml of beer
- ½ g saffron
- 1 sprig of rosemary
- 1 sprig of thyme
- 250g of bomba rice

For the *Alioli*
- 30g mayonnaise
- 1 clove of garlic, crushed

Method

1. Boil 200ml of water. Add the mussels, white wine, peppercorns, ground pepper and bay leaf to a saucepan and bring to a simmer. Add the boiled water, cover with a lid and simmer for 3 – 5 minutes, or until the mussels open. Don't overcook as the mussels will go rubbery. Remove from the heat and set aside to cool a bit. Lift out the mussels and remove the top half of the shells. Discard any mussels that haven't opened. Set the mussels aside.
2. Strain the mussel cooking liquid into a large jug or saucepan.

Crumble in the seafood stock cubes and add enough boiling water to make 600ml of stock. Stir until the stock cubes have dissolved. Set aside the seafood stock.

3. Add all the tomato sauce ingredients to a blender and process until smooth. Set aside.

4. Add 3 tablespoons of extra virgin olive oil to a paella pan, or a large pan, over high heat. Add the prawn heads and sauté for a few minutes, constantly stirring with a wooden spoon to ensure they are nicely browned all over. Squeeze the prawn heads well with the spoon to extract as much flavour as you can from them. Remove the prawn heads from the pan and discard.

5. Add the prawn tails to the pan and cook over high heat for 1 minute each side. Remove the prawns and set aside.

6. Add the diced chicken to the pan over high heat, season with a pinch of salt and black pepper and fry until golden. Reduce the heat to medium and cook for a further 5 minutes.

7. Add the tomato puree, the paprika powder and the prepared tomato sauce and cook for further 8 minutes.

8. Add the beer and cook until the beer has almost completely reduced.

9. Add, the rosemary, thyme, a pinch of salt and the rice. Stir for a couple of minutes so that the rice absorbs all the pan flavours.

10. Turn the heat to high and add the prepared seafood stock to the pan. Add the saffron and stir to distribute the rice evenly across the pan.

11. Once the liquid comes to the boil don't stir the rice again. Cook on medium-high heat for a further 10 minutes.

12. Reduce the heat to medium and add the prawns and mussels in a decorative way and cook for a further 8 minutes. Remember not to stir the rice!

13. Remove the pan from the heat and cover with aluminium foil or a cloth. Set aside for 5 minutes so that the rice continues to be cooked by the steam.
14. While the paella is steaming prepare the *alioli*. Add the mayonnaise and crushed garlic to a small bowl and stir until the garlic is well mixed with the mayonnaise.
15. Serve the paella in separate dishes or place the pan in the centre of the table so that people can serve themselves.

Tip

Quarter a lemon and place the quarters on the side of the rice dish, or on a small dish, so that people add lemon to their rice if they wish.

Arroz con Pollo – Rice with Chicken

This is a simple way of making a nice rice dish if you don't have much time or ingredients available. Sometimes less is more! It is always best to use free-range or organic chicken and have the *arroz* (rice) with a salad.

Difficulty: easy
Prep time: 10 min
Cooking time: 25 min
Serves: 4
Special equipment: blender

Ingredients

For the tomato sauce
- 2 garlic cloves
- 1 tomato
- ½ red bell pepper, diced
- pinch of sea salt

For the rice
- 2 organic chicken stock cubes
- 3 tablespoons of extra virgin olive oil
- 200g deboned, skinless chicken thighs, diced in 2cm pieces
- ½ teaspoon *La Vera* smoked paprika powder
- 250g of bomba rice
- sea salt
- ½ g saffron
- 1 sprig of rosemary
- 1 sprig of thyme

Method

1. Add all the tomato sauce ingredients to a blender and process until smooth. Set aside.
2. Crumble the chicken stock cubes into a jug or saucepan. Add 600ml of boiling water and stir until the stock cubes have dissolved. Set aside.
3. Add 3 tablespoons of extra virgin olive oil to a paella pan, or large pan, over high heat. Add the chicken and sauté until golden.
4. Reduce the heat to medium. Add the paprika and prepared tomato sauce to the chicken and cook for a further 5 minutes.
5. Add the rice and a pinch of salt and stir the rice for a couple of minutes so that the rice absorbs all the pan flavours.
6. Turn the heat to high and add the prepared chicken stock to the pan. Add the saffron and stir to distribute the rice evenly across the pan.
7. Place the rosemary and the thyme on the rice. Once the liquid comes to the boil don't stir the rice again. Cook on medium-high heat for a further 10 minutes.
8. Reduce the heat to medium and cook for a further 4 minutes. Then, reduce the heat to very low and cook for another 3 minutes. Remember not to stir the rice!
9. Remove the pan from the heat and cover with aluminium foil or a cloth. Set aside for 5 minutes so that the rice continues to be cooked by the steam.
10. Serve the paella in separate dishes or place the pan in the centre of the table so that people can serve themselves.

Tip

Quarter a lemon and place the quarters on the side of the rice dish, or on a small dish, so that people add lemon to their rice if they wish.

Arroz Negro – Black Rice

I love making this dish when I really want to reminisce about my times in Spain. It brings flavours of the sea together and reminds me of being on holiday.

Difficulty: easy
Prep time: 10 min
Cooking time: 25 min
Serves: 4
Special equipment: blender

Ingredients

For the tomato sauce
- 2 garlic cloves
- 1 tomato
- ½ red bell pepper, diced
- pinch of sea salt

For the rice
- 2 seafood stock cubes
- 3 sachets of cuttlefish ink
- 3 tablespoons of extra virgin olive oil
- 8 king prawns, heads removed (keep the heads) & tails de-shelled
- 200g squid
- ½ teaspoon *La Vera* smoked paprika powder
- 250g of bomba rice
- ½ g saffron
- sea salt

For the *Alioli* sauce
- 30g mayonnaise
- 1 clove of garlic, crushed

Method

1. Add all the tomato sauce ingredients to a blender and process until smooth. Set aside.
2. Crumble the seafood stock cubes into a jug or saucepan. Add 600ml of boiling water and stir until the stock cubes have dissolved. Stir the sachets of cuttlefish ink into the seafood stock. Set aside.
3. Wash the squid and dry with kitchen paper roll. Cut into small pieces. Set aside.
4. Add 3 tablespoons of extra virgin olive oil to a paella pan, or a large pan, over high heat. Add the prawn heads and sauté for a few minutes, constantly stirring with a wooden spoon to ensure they are nicely browned all over. Squeeze the prawn heads well with the spoon to extract as much flavour as you can from them. Remove the prawn heads from the pan and discard.
5. Add the prawn tails to the pan. Cook over high heat for 1 minute on each side. Remove the prawns and set aside.
6. Add the squid to the pan over high heat, season with salt and fry for a minute or two until golden all over.
7. Reduce the heat to medium. Add the paprika and prepared tomato sauce to the squid and cook for a further 5 minutes.
8. Add the rice and a pinch of salt and stir the rice for a couple of minutes so that the rice absorbs all the pan flavours.

9. Turn the heat to high and add the prepared seafood stock to the pan. Add the saffron and stir to distribute the rice evenly across the pan.

10. Once the liquid comes to the boil don't stir the rice again. Cook on medium-high heat for a further 10 minutes.

11. Reduce the heat to medium. Add the prawns in a decorative way and cook for a further 4 minutes. Reduce the heat to very low and continue to cook for a further 3 minutes. Remember not to stir the rice!

12. Remove the pan from the heat and cover with aluminium foil or a cloth. Set aside for 5 minutes so that the rice continues to be cooked by the steam.

13. While the paella is steaming prepare the *alioli* to serve with the paella. Add the mayonnaise and crushed garlic to a small bowl and stir until the garlic is well mixed with the mayonnaise.

14. Serve the paella in 4 separate dishes or place the pan in the centre of the table so that people can serve themselves. You can also serve it in 8 dishes as a tapa.

Tip

Quarter a lemon and place the quarters on the side of the rice dish, or on a small dish, so that people add lemon to their rice if they wish.

Arroz con Pollo y Verduras - Rice with Chicken & Vegetables

This is one of my papa's recipes! Originally from Castilla la Mancha, it brings back memories of good times with family and friends in Spain. You only need a large kitchen pan for this recipe. We usually make a salad to serve with the paella.

Difficulty: easy
Prep time: 10 min
Cooking time: 25 min
Serves: 4 people

Ingredients

- 3 tablespoons extra virgin olive oil
- 1 organic skinless chicken thigh, diced into 2 cm pieces
- 1 clove of unpeeled garlic, halved
- 2 cloves of garlic, finely diced
- 1 tomato, chopped (or ½ can chopped tomato)
- ½ red bell pepper, diced
- ½ green bell pepper, diced
- sea salt
- 4 asparagus spears, sliced into 1 cm pieces
- 1 dried chilli
- 2 organic chicken stock cubes
- 1 sachet (3 g) of paella spice mix (I use Carmencita Paellero)
- 250g of bomba rice

Method

1. Add 3 tablespoons of olive oil to a large pan over high heat. Add the chicken and sauté until golden all over. Add both the 2 halves of skin-on garlic and the diced garlic to the chicken and sauté for another minute.
2. Add the chopped tomatoes, bell peppers and a pinch of salt. Crush the chilli with your hands into the pan. Reduce the heat to medium and continue to cook until the bell peppers have softened. Add the asparagus and continue to cook for another 2 minutes.
3. Turn the heat to high and add 600ml of tap water to the pan. Crumble the stock cubes with your fingers into the water and add the paella spice. Stir until the water comes to the boil and the stock cubes have dissolved.
4. Now add the rice to the pan like this: start in the centre of the pan and then evenly pour the rice in a circular motion moving outwards towards the edge of the pan. Don't stir the rice once in the pan. Cook on medium-high heat for 10 minutes.
5. Reduce the temperature to low and cook for a further 10 minutes.
6. Serve the paella in 4 separate dishes or place the pan in the centre of the table so that people can serve themselves.

Tip

Quarter a lemon and place the quarters on the side of the rice dish, or on a small dish, so that people add lemon to their rice if they wish.

Arroz con Marsico de Julio - Julio's Rice with Seafood

This is one of my papa's recipes. I love it because it is so easy to make and is very delicious with a spicy touch.

Difficulty: easy
Prep time: 10 min
Cooking time: 25 min
Serves: 4 people

Ingredients

For the vegetable stock
- 8 cleaned mussels (we only need 4 but we have more in case they don't open)
- 50ml of white wine
- 4 black peppercorns
- freshly ground black pepper, to taste
- 1 bay leaf

For the rice
- 200g squid, cut into small pieces
- 3 tablespoons of extra virgin olive oil
- 1 clove of unpeeled garlic, halved
- 2 cloves of garlic, finely diced
- 1 tomato, chopped (or ½ can chopped tomato)
- ½ red bell pepper, diced
- ½ green bell pepper, diced
- sea salt
- 4 asparagus spears, sliced into 1 cm pieces
- 1 dried chilli
- 2 organic vegetable stock cubes
- 1 sachet (3 g) paella spice mix

- 250g of bomba rice
- 4 king prawns

Method

1. Boil 200ml of water. Add the mussels, white wine, peppercorns, ground pepper and bay leaf to a saucepan and bring to a simmer. Add the boiled water, cover with a lid and simmer for 3 – 5 minutes, or until the mussels open. Don't overcook as the mussels will go rubbery. Remove from the heat and strain the mussels, reserving the liquid for later. Remove the top half of the mussel shells. Discard any mussels that haven't opened. Set aside.
2. Wash and dry the squid with kitchen paper roll.
3. Add 3 tablespoons of olive oil to a large pan over high heat. Add the squid and sauté until golden all over. Add both the 2 halves of skin-on garlic and the diced garlic to the squid and sauté for another couple of minutes.
4. Add the chopped tomatoes, bell peppers and a pinch of salt. Crush the chilli with your hands into the pan. Reduce the heat to medium and continue to cook until the bell peppers have softened. Add the asparagus and continue to cook for another 2 minutes.
5. Turn the heat to high. Add enough tap water to the reserved mussel liquid to make up 600ml of stock and add to the pan. Crumble the stock cubes with your fingers into the water and add the paella spice. Stir until the water comes to the boil and the stock cubes have dissolved.
6. Now add the rice to the pan like this: start in the centre of the pan and then evenly pour the rice in a circular motion moving outwards towards the edge of the pan.

Don't stir the rice once in the pan. Cook on medium-high heat for 10 minutes.

7. Reduce the heat to low and add the mussels and prawns in a decorative way and cook for a further 10 minutes.

8. Serve the paella in 4 separate dishes or place the pan in the centre of the table so that people can serve themselves. You can also serve it in 8 dishes as a tapa.

Tip

Quarter a lemon and place the quarters on the side of the rice dish, or on a small dish, so that people add lemon to their rice if they wish.

FISH & SEAFOOD

Madrid, despite being inland in the middle of Spain, has the freshest fish. This is because there is a huge demand for fresh, good quality fish from the many bars and restaurants located in Madrid. Fresh fish is delivered directly from the coast of Spain to the supermarkets every morning. You can smell the freshness of the fish in the markets and the variety on offer is huge. You can find the most spectacular seafood dishes in bars and restaurants of the capital, as well as in the other inland regions of Spain.

Mejillones a la Marinera – Galician Style Mussels with White Wine

This recipe brings you the seafood flavours of Galicia, on the north coast of Spain, where 95% of the mussels in Spain comes from. This meal is very tasty and healthy as mussels contain a high amount of protein and are low in fat. I love preparing this dish for special occasions as it looks very classy and good to show off with!

Difficulty: easy
Prep time: 5 min
Cooking time: 20 min
Serves: 4

Ingredients

- 3kg mussels
- 7 bay leaves
- sea salt
- 3 tablespoons of extra virgin olive oil
- 3 diced onions
- 2 tablespoons of chopped parsley
- 3 tablespoons of flour (you can use gluten free or any other flour you like)
- 250ml mussel stock (water that the mussels were cooked in)
- 250ml white wine (Galician wine such as Albariño if possible)
- 1 tablespoon La Vera sweet paprika powder

Method

1. Clean the mussels by scrubbing the shell and pulling away the "beards". Rinse with cold water.
2. Bring a 100ml of water to the boil in a large saucepan over high heat. Add 1 tablespoon of salt, the bay leaves and the mussels. Put the lid and cook the mussels until the shells open, approximately 3 minutes. Remove the mussels and discard any mussels that have not opened. Set aside.
3. Strain the stock from the saucepan and keep it to use later. Return the remaining mussels to the saucepan.
4. To make the sauce heat 3 tablespoons of extra virgin olive oil in a large pan over medium heat. Add the onion and sauté until softened and golden. Add the chopped parsley and flour and stir until the flour is nicely browned. Add the strained mussel stock, wine and paprika to the pan. Cook for a couple of minutes, stirring occasionally.
5. Add the sauce from the pan to the mussels in the saucepan and cook for 2 minutes, stirring until the sauce has thickened.
6. Turn off the heat and leave it for a couple of minutes before serving.

Tip

Serve the mussels in a terracotta dish if you have one as it'll look more authentic.

Pimientos de Piquillo Rellenos - Stuffed Piquillo Peppers

Difficulty: easy
Prep time: 10 min
Cooking time: 45 min
Serves: 4

Ingredients

- 120ml extra virgin olive oil
- 1 onion, diced
- 1 green bell pepper, diced
- 2 chillies, diced
- 4 garlic cloves, diced
- 2 cans (400g cans) of chopped tomato
- 400g baby squid
- sea salt
- 12 (about 260g) piquillo peppers, drained

Method

1. Add the olive oil to a large pan over medium-high heat. When hot, add the onion and cook for a couple of minutes before adding the bell pepper. Continue to cook until the onions and peppers are soft.
2. Add the chilies and the garlic and cook for a further 5 minutes.
3. Add the 2 cans of chopped tomatoes and continue to cook for another 10 minutes over medium heat.
4. While the tomato sauce is cooking rinse the squid with cold water. Add them to the tomato sauce and season with a pinch of salt. Cook for a further 10 minutes.

5. Stuff the piquillo peppers with the squid and some tomato sauce, leaving the remaining tomato sauce in the pan. Arrange the stuffed piquillo peppers in a decorative way in the pan with the sauce.

Lubina Rebozada - Battered Sea Bass

This is also a common method of cooking fish, popular in Spanish households, schools and restaurants.

Difficulty: easy
Prep time: 5 min
Cooking time: 10 min
Serves: 4

Ingredients

- 4 sea bass fillets, cut in half to get 8 pieces
- 125g flour (you can use gluten free or any other flour you like)
- 2 eggs
- extra virgin olive oil
- freshly ground black pepper
- sea salt
- juice of 1 lemon

Method

1. Clean the fish with cold water and dry with kitchen paper roll.
2. Add the flour to a baking tray. Whisk the eggs in a bowl.
3. Dip the fish into the flour, ensuring you coat both sides well with flour. Shake off any excess flour. Then dip the floured fish into the whisked egg, ensuring you cover the fish well all over with whisked egg.
4. Heat a large pan over medium-high heat with a generous amount of olive oil.

When the oil is hot, add the battered fish fillets to the pan and fry for 4 - 5 minutes on each side, or until golden. If needed you can fry the fish in two batches.

5. Line a bowl with a few layers of kitchen paper roll. Place the fried fish on the kitchen paper roll to drain excess oil.
6. Let the fish cool a bit before placing in a serving dish. Season with salt, black pepper and lemon juice.

Tip

It's great to accompany the fish with any one of the salads from the salad section.

Sardinas al Horno - Roasted Sardines

I love having sardines, especially for dinner because they make for a very light meal and are healthy full of Omega 3. The best quality sardines are available from May to October. They need feel firm to touch and smell fresh and the eyes must be shiny, not cloudy and yellow. This dish is very popular on the south coast of Spain. They are very quick and easy to cook in the oven and served with a salad or vegetables.

Difficulty: easy
Prep time: 15 min
Cooking time: 15 min
Serves: 4

Ingredients

- 500g sardines
- coarse salt
- 1 lemon

Method

1. Preheat the oven to 220° C.
2. Clean the sardines with cold water, cut open the belly and remove the innards using your thumb. Dry with kitchen paper roll.
3. Line a baking tray with baking paper and sprinkle evenly with a layer of coarse salt. Place the sardines on the salt in a single layer. Don't place a sardine on another sardine.
4. Cover the sardines with another sprinkling of coarse salt.

5. Place the tray in the middle of the oven and cook for 15 minutes. The sardines are done if the skin comes away easily and the inside of the sardine is cooked through and juicy. If the inside is still a bit raw continue to cook them for another 5 minutes, or until cooked.
6. Served with lemon pieces.

POULTRY & MEAT

Cocido Madrileño – Madrid Style Chickpea Stew

Cocido is a traditional meat and chickpea-based stew from Madrid. My papa's recipe is made with chorizo, pork and beef. As this is a dish is heavy on the meat and rich, we normally only eat it on special occasions and we also always serve it with a salad to create a freshness to the meal.

Difficulty: easy
Prep time: 20 min
Cooking time: 1 hour
Serves: 4

Ingredients

- 4 big handfuls of chickpeas, soaked in water overnight
- 2 large pieces of beef shin
- 2 dried ham bones
- 1 pork tail, cut in half
- 4 raw chorizo sausages
- 2 peeled carrots, diced
- 2 thick slices of *Iberico panceta* (or cured pork belly or pancetta)
- 2 peeled potatoes cut into halves

Method

1. Wash all the meat with water.
2. Add the drained chickpeas, carrots, beef shins, ham bones, pork tail, chorizo and lard to a pot over high heat.

Fill the pot with water up to the top and bring to the boil uncovered. As the oil and impurities rise to the surface skim it off with a skimming spoon.

3. Continue occasionally skimming off the oil rising to the surface. When no more oil rises to the surface, reduce the heat to medium and cover the pot with a lid. Cook for 1 hour.
4. Add the potatoes and cook for another 30 minutes.
5. Serve the cocido in four dishes as a main meal or place the pot in the centre of the table so that people can serve themselves.

Tip

The traditional way to eat this dish is to remove the meat and vegetables from the pot to a serving dish. You then cook broken vermicelli in the stock for 10 minutes and serve it as a soup first and then you serve the meat and vegetables after, separately in a sharing dish.

Pollo al Ajillo - Chicken in Garlic Sauce

Pollo al ajillo is a classic Spanish recipe originally from Andalucía, but it is enjoyed in all regions of Spain. Every family has their own version, but ours is made with a combination of wine, garlic and beer which makes this a unique dish. As this is a meat-based recipe, we always serve a vegetable salad alongside to create a healthier meal.

Difficulty: easy
Prep time: 10 min
Cooking time: 30 min
Serves: 4

Ingredients

- 2 tablespoons of extra virgin olive oil
- 500g skinless chicken, diced
- 5 small garlic cloves with skin on, cut in half
- sea salt
- black pepper
- 1 dried chilli
- 100ml white wine
- 1 onion, diced

For the sauce

- 4 large garlic cloves, peeled
- coarse salt
- 3 tablespoons of extra virgin olive oil
- 330ml lager beer
- 3 tablespoons of white wine vinegar
- Special equipment: pestle & mortar

Method

1. Heat a large pan with 2 tablespoons of extra virgin olive oil over a medium-high heat. When hot, add the diced chicken, the 5 halved, skin-on garlic cloves, a pinch of sea salt and black pepper.
2. While the chicken is cooking, crush the 4 large garlic cloves and a pinch of coarse salt with a pestle and mortar. Then add 3 tablespoons of olive oil and 3 tablespoons of white wine vinegar to the mortar and mix.
3. Once the chicken is golden and almost done, crush the chilli with your fingers into the pan and add the onion. Cook for 2 minutes and then add the white wine. Simmer until the liquid is reduced by half.
4. Add some beer to the contents of the mortar and mix. When the onion is soft add the contents of the mortar to the pan. Rinse the mortar with some more beer and add to the pan.
5. Continue to cook the chicken for about another 2 minutes before adding the remaining beer and a small glass of hot water to cover the chicken. Continue simmering until the sauce has thickened.
6. Serve the chicken in four dishes as a main meal or place the pan in the centre of the table so that people can serve themselves.

Tip

Quarter a lemon and place the quarters on a small dish so that people add lemon to their chicken if they wish.

Caldereta de Cordero - Lamb Stew

This is one of my favourite dishes when visiting my papa's hometown in Cuenca, Castilla la Mancha. It is a little village called Villamayor de Santiago. We usually meet friends and family at our homes and make this dish outdoors on a fire, but we also cook it at home in Madrid in our kitchen. The variety of flavours is just delicious. Combine any salad or vegetables from the salad or side dishes sections with the stew to create some freshness to the meal.

Difficulty: easy
Prep time: 10 min
Cooking time: 30 min
Serves: 4

Ingredients

- 2 ½ kg diced lamb leg
- 4 garlic cloves cut in half
- ½ red bell pepper, diced
- ½ green bell pepper, diced
- 1 white onion, diced
- 2 chillies
- 2 bay leaves
- salt
- black pepper
- 330ml of white wine
- 200ml of whiskey

Method

1. Place the meat into a hot saucepan over high heat. Add enough boiled water to cover the meat and add a pinch of salt.
2. Once it is the water has come to the boil drain the water from the pot, leaving the lamb in the saucepan.
3. Add the garlic, red bell pepper, green bell pepper, onion, chillies and the bay leaves to the lamb. Add some salt and pepper and place the saucepan over a high heat. Add the white wine and whisky and enough boiled water to cover the lamb.
4. Simmer the lamb until the sauce has thickened.

Filletes de Carrilladas - Pork Cheek Fillets

This dish is also popular in Castilla la Mancha. Pork cheeks are tender and full of flavour. Combine any salad or vegetables from the salad or side dishes sections to add freshness.

Difficulty: easy
Prep time: 10 min
Cooking time: 30 min
Serves: 4

Ingredients

- 8 pork cheek fillets
- 4 small garlic cloves (leave the skin on)
- 2 tablespoons of extra virgin olive oil

For the marinade
- 1 garlic head
- 2 dried chillies
- 4 tablespoons of extra virgin olive oil
- 4 tablespoons of white wine vinegar
- coarse salt
- black pepper
- Special Equipment: pestle & mortar

Method

1. Start by preparing the meat by slicing the fillets horizontally and then making small incisions around the edge of the meat to avoid it shrinking and curling during the cooking process.
2. Remove 4 garlic cloves from the middle of the head of garlic head and cut each in half, leaving the skin on.

3. Peel and dice the remaining head of garlic. Add the garlic along with the chillies, a pinch of coarse salt and black pepper to a mortar and crush the garlic and chillies. Add 4 tablespoons of extra virgin olive oil and 4 tablespoons of white vinegar to the mortar and mix.
4. Coat the pork with the marinade from the mortar and marinate in a dish for 10 minutes. Remove the pork from the marinade and scrape off any marinade sticking to the fillets back into the dish. Keep the marinade.
5. Heat a large pan with 2 tablespoons of extra virgin olive oil over a high heat. Once hot add the skin-on garlic halves and the pork fillets. If needed you can fry the fillets in batches. Try to avoid adding pieces of garlic from the marinade to the pan at this stage as garlic without skin on burns quickly.
6. Once the fillets are nicely browned underneath turn them over and cook them for half the time than the other side. If cooking the fillets in batches remove the first batch from the pan to a dish and cook the next batch.
7. Add the marinade to the pan. If necessary, rinse the mortar with a little vinegar and add residue to the pan. Cook the marinade for a minute or two. Add the fillets to the pan, coat with marinade and cook until done.
8. Serve the pork check fillets in four dishes as a main meal or the pan in the centre of the table so that people can serve themselves.

Tip

Quarter a lemon and place the quarters on a small dish so that people add lemon to their chicken if they wish.

Magro con Tomate - Pork with Tomato Sauce

This pork stew recipe is a simple dish but full of flavour. It is originally from Navarra in the north of Spain but is very popular elsewhere in Spain, either in restaurants or at home. *Magro* means meat with no fat.

Difficulty: easy
Prep time: 10 min
Cooking time: 30 min
Serves: 4

Ingredients

- 500g cubed stewing pork
- salt
- black pepper
- 2 tablespoons of extra virgin olive oil
- 1 white onion, diced
- 3 garlic cloves, diced
- 1 green bell pepper, diced
- 200ml of white wine
- 2 cans of chopped tomatoes or 1kg diced fresh tomatoes
- 1 bay leaf
- 2 teaspoons of sugar

Method

1. Place the meat in a bowl, season with salt and pepper and leave it at room temperature for 30 minutes.
2. Heat a large pan over a medium-high heat and add the olive oil.

When hot, add the pork and stir-fry until nicely browned all over and almost done. Remove the pork from the pan to a dish and set aside.

3. Reduce the heat to low. Add the onion, garlic and bell pepper to the same pan that you cooked the pork in and cook for 10 minutes, until the onion and bell pepper are soft. Increase the heat and add the wine. Cook for further 2 to 3 minutes.

4. Reduce the heat to low and add the chopped tomatoes, bay leaf and sugar to the pan and cook for a further 30 minutes.

5. Remove the bay leaf from the tomato sauce. Pour the tomato sauce into a food processor, or blender, and process until smooth. Add the sauce back to the pan.

6. Add the pork to the sauce and warm it over low heat before serving.

7. Serve the pork with tomato in four dishes as a main meal or the pan in the centre of the table so that people can serve themselves.

TIPS FROM ME

You can combine any of these recipes to prepare delicious and special meals that are different to what you usually cook. Treat yourself or surprise your loved ones on special occasions. But you can also use these recipes for your daily or weekday meals by combining fish or meat main dishes with side dishes and salads. You can be sure that these meals are healthy if you prepare them properly. If you prepare enough you can have meals for a few days. You can maybe leave the tapas and rice dishes for weekends so that you can share them while socialising with friends, just as we do in Spain.

Spending time with friends and family is the most important thing for us and sharing a meal is our favourite way of socialising.

With these recipes you can have a variety of meals for a year without having to think too much of what to cook next. A typical meal I love to prepare for lunch is the chicken in garlic sauce with grilled wild asparagus. I also like making roasted sardines with bonito tuna and piquillo peppers salad for dinner. Or even a battered sea bass with a Mediterranean tuna salad.

I usually have more time to cook on weekends and I make more filling dishes like fried potatoes with courgettes and garlic, and pork cheek fillets with salad. But if you batch cook the potatoes and the pork cheeks you can have some for the weekdays too.

Pisto is a great meal to batch cook. You can keep the vegetables in the fridge for a few days and you just need to fry a couple of eggs each time you have it. You can also combine it with fish or meat dishes. Rice meals are my favourites for weekends and we usually make a nice salad to complete the meal.

I like making cocido (for special occasions only) as well as lamb stew.

Spanish omelette is always a great option for dinner especially combined with padrón peppers or gazpacho and if I have any leftovers, I happily have it for breakfast with my coffee. In fact, *pincho de tortilla*, which is Spanish omelette with bread is a common breakfast meal in Spanish cafés.

You can combine tapas as you like, and you can also make a meal with them. You often have them on social occasions but sometimes, when I am not really that hungry, I take the jamón and the cheese out of the fridge and have a small nibble together with a piece of fruit. Spanish cooking is all about that, simplicity but with great flavours.

From the bottom of my heart, thanks for buying my cookbook and I hope you enjoy these meals as much as I do and that you share them with the people you love the most. I'd appreciate if you could leave a review on Amazon as I'd love to hear from you soon!

Love Vanesa x

Click here to leave a review for this book on Amazon!

BONUS

If you like these recipes and want special, free recipes please click here, or go to my website www.vanesamaza.com_to get instant access to these incredible free tools and resources.

Printed by Amazon Italia Logistica S.r.l.
Torrazza Piemonte (TO), Italy

36703333R00067